TRAVEL MATH

Math and My World

Kieran Walsh

Rourke
Publishing LLC
Vero Beach, Florida 32964

www.rourkepublishing.com

PHOTO CREDITS:
Cover photo by PictureQuest.com. All other photos from AbleStock.com, except for pages 12, 16, 20 by the author and illustration of a family inside a car © Getty Images

Editor: Frank Sloan

Cover and interior design by Nicola Stratford
Page layout by Heather Scarborough

Library of Congress Cataloging-in-Publication Data

Walsh, Kieran.
Travel math / by Kieran Walsh.
p. cm. -- (Math and my world)
Includes bibliographical references and index.
Contents: Walking -- The speedometer -- Miles per hour -- Trains -- Planes -- The Concorde -- Sound and light -- Space planes.
ISBN 1-58952-383-0 (hardcover)
1. Mathematics--Study and teaching (Elementary)--Juvenile literature. 2. Travel--Juvenile literature. [1. Mathematics. 2. Travel.] I. Title. II. Series: Walsh, Kieran. Math and my world.
QA135.6.W34 2003
629.04--dc22

2003011563

Printed in the USA

w/w

TABLE OF CONTENTS

INTRODUCTION

What does the word **travel** mean to you?

In fact, all travel really means is to go from one place to another. Traveling is something people do all the time, both in small ways and big ways.

A means of traveling, or from getting from one place to another, is a form of **transportation**. Can you name a few forms of transportation?

Probably the ones that spring to mind are cars, trains, and planes. For instance, when you take the bus to school, you are traveling. But did you know that **escalators** are also a form of transportation? Of course, escalators don't take you very far, but they still move you from one place to another.

Despite the fact that they don't take you very far, even escalators are a form of transportation.

In this book, you're going to learn about different types of transportation. You will also learn about the differences between these types of transportation.

You see, not all forms of transportation are equal. The key difference between forms of transportation is **speed**, in other words, what method of travel will get you to your destination the quickest. To figure out the fastest way to get from one place to another, you are going to use math to compare the different forms of transportation.

What would you guess is the slowest form of transportation?

Probably the slowest form of transportation is something you do every day—walking!

Did you know that when you walk from one classroom to another you are using a form of transportation?

WALKING

When was the last time you took a nice, long walk?

These days, walking is generally thought of as a form of **recreation** or **exercise**. Walking, though, is really the most basic form of transportation human beings have. In fact, walking is the one form of transportation a human being can take advantage of without needing any other equipment.

One of the fastest animals on the planet, a cheetah can run at speeds up to 60 miles per hour. Part of the reason why animals like the cheetah are faster than humans is because they have four legs.

Walking isn't taken very seriously any more as a form of transportation simply because we have many other, far more **efficient**, ways to travel from one place to another. Cars, trains, and planes are all faster than walking.

This has probably raised an interesting question in your mind. Just how fast is walking?

The first thing to do would be to find out how many steps you take in one minute. You may need to use a stopwatch or some other form of timer to do this. Your results will vary, but just to demonstrate the math, let's say that you took 60 steps in one minute.

What this means will become clearer when you multiply 60 by 2. The 2 stands for *two feet.* This is the average **stride length**, or the distance a person covers with a single step.

Stride length varies from person to person. One way to measure your exact stride length is to set a distance, 10 feet, for instance, and see how many steps it takes you to walk that length.

$$60 \times 2 = 120$$

Now you know that in one minute you walk a distance of roughly 120 feet.

Using this information, can you calculate how long it would take you to walk one mile?

The mile is the basis of length in the U.S. Customary System of measurement, also known as the English System of measurement. One mile is equal to roughly 5,280 feet. If you walk at a pace of about 120 feet per minute, you can find out how long it would take you to travel a mile by using division:

$$5{,}280 \div 120 = 44$$

So, to walk a length of one mile, it would take you about 44 minutes.

How does that sound to you? Not too bad?

Okay, but what if your destination, the place you have to go, is 20 miles away? How long would it take you to get there by walking?

You can find out by multiplying the time it takes to travel one mile by the number of miles:

$$20 \times 44 = 880$$

It would take about 880 minutes to travel a distance of 20 miles on foot. To convert that number to hours, you can divide it by 60, which is the number of minutes in one hour:

$$880 \div 60 = 14.6$$

Wow! To walk a distance of 20 miles would take about 15 hours!

For traveling great distances, walking is simply not efficient. How long, for instance, would it take you to walk a mile at your stride length? What about 15 miles?

That number really puts things in perspective, and it probably makes sense to you now why people worked to develop easier, more efficient forms of travel. The relatively slow speed of walking led to the invention of the form of transport you are probably most familiar with, the automobile.

The Pedometer

For the most accurate measure of your walking speed, you would need to use a pedometer. A pedometer is actually a combination of two devices—a pendulum and a calculator. The pendulum swings each time it feels the vibrations from your feet hitting the ground. Meanwhile, the calculator divides the number of steps you take by 5,280—the number of feet in one mile. Because a pedometer depends on vibrations to count your steps, it is not good for measuring distances covered by activities that do not involve impact, like bike riding.

THE SPEEDOMETER

Have you ever looked at the **dashboard** of your family's car? Maybe you have seen it from the passenger's seat on the right, but have you ever sat on the left?

This is the view of the inside of your family's car you are probably familiar with. But what do you see if you sit on the left?

From the driver's seat, a car dashboard looks much more complicated. There are lights that blink, needles that jump, and lots of numbers.

The numbers we're interested in, though, are located on an instrument just above the steering wheel. This particular instrument is called a **speedometer**. As you may have guessed, a speedometer is used to tell the speed at which a car is traveling.

Your speedometer will have a series of numbers that look something like this:

20 40 60 80 100 120

Obviously, these are not your standard 1, 2, 3, 4 numbers. These numbers are **multiples**.

You have already dealt with multiples if you have ever practiced your **multiplication** tables. For example, have you ever done the multiples of 5? Try it now:

0 x 5 = 0
1 x 5 = 5
2 x 5 = 10
3 x 5 = 15
4 x 5 = 20
...and so on.

The labeled numbers on a speedometer are also multiples. To be precise, they are multiples of *twenty*:

0 x 20 = 0
1 x 20 = 20
2 x 20 = 40
3 x 20 = 60
4 x 20 = 80
5 x 20 = 100
... and so on.

Note that the *labeled* numbers on a speedometer are multiples of 20. That is because a speedometer also contains a lot of invisible numbers. Take a closer look at the speedometer. For instance, between 20 and 40 there are some lines, or **notches**, that are not given numbers—what do they represent?

A speedometer looks a little bit like the face of a clock. Can you determine what speeds the unmarked notches on this speedometer represent?

It's really very simple. Just as the labeled numbers are multiples of 20, the notches that are not labeled are multiples of 5. So, in between 20 and 40 are three hidden numbers:

20 *25* *30* *35* 40

Another way to look at a speedometer is to say that each notch is a multiple of 5, but only the multiples of 20 are labeled.

Speedometers are set up this way for convenience. If a speedometer included every single number from 0 to 120, it would have to be pretty big, and it would be very hard to read!

!

The Odometer

Within the speedometer can be found another device called an odometer. The purpose of the odometer is to measure the number of miles covered in a journey. That is why odometers come with a "reset" button that allows you to set it back to zero at the start of a new trip. Although digital, or computerized, odometers are becoming more popular, old-fashioned gear odometers are still very common. A gear odometer registers one mile after spinning 1,690 times. Can you calculate how many times the gear of an odometer would spin for a trip of 15 miles?

MILES PER HOUR

In the last section you started to learn about the numbers on a speedometer. In this section, you're going to learn about what those numbers mean.

If you look closely at the speedometer again, you'll see that it is labeled not only with numbers, but letters. Somewhere on the speedometer you will find letters that read MPH. Perhaps you know already what these letters stand for: *miles per hour.*

Miles per hour is a unit of measurement much like the feet per minute calculation you did in the section on walking. Of course, a car covers a much greater distance in a shorter period of time than a person walking, which is why the standard is miles per hour, rather than feet per minute.

You probably also remember the imaginary example you used to determine how long it would take for a person to walk a distance of 20 miles.

Let's try that calculation again. This time, though, you're going to get to your destination by car. More specifically, you'll be in a car traveling at 20 miles per hour. How long would it take to get to your destination now?

$$20 \div 20 = 1$$

If you were in a car traveling at an average speed of 60 MPH, how long would it take you to travel a distance of 1,150 miles?

So, in a car traveling at 20 miles per hour, it would take *1 hour* to travel a distance of 20 miles. That's a big improvement over the 15 hours it would take to walk the same distance. It's also important to note that, for the most part, a car can travel much faster than 20 miles per hour. In reality you could travel a distance of 20 miles in about 15 minutes. That's quite an improvement!

And that is exactly what is meant by the term *efficiency.* Cars are simply more *efficient* forms of travel than walking. Cars help people get to where they need to go quickly.

The speedometer is not only useful for determining how long it will take to get somewhere. It is also an important tool for figuring how the speed of a car being driven compares to the **speed limit** of a stretch of road.

Speed limits are not randomly selected. They are chosen because they are thought to be the safest speed for that particular stretch of road. Speed limits can go up and down depending on a number of different factors including the path of the road, the weather conditions of a particular area, and the population density of the area the road travels through. For instance, on a **highway** that passes by a stretch of bare land, the speed limit might be 65 mph. In a **residential** area where children might play, though, a typical speed might be 30 mph.

Because speed limits are extremely important for safety, the police will often stop people who are not traveling at a speed close to the speed limit. That is why the speedometer is useful for making sure that you are traveling at the required speed.

Let's say you are driving in an area with a speed limit of 30 mph, but the speedometer indicates that you are driving at 45 mph. How many miles per hour over the speed limit are you traveling?

You can find out by using subtraction:

$$45 - 30 = 15$$

You are traveling 15 miles per hour above the speed limit. This kind of behavior, known as *speeding*, can get you pulled over by the police.

Policemen also take notice, though, if you are driving too slowly. Slow driving might be safe, but it can be an annoyance to other drivers on the road.

What if you are in a car that is traveling 40 miles per hour on a highway with a speed limit of 65 miles per hour? How much slower are you driving compared to the speed limit? To find out, just subtract the smaller number from the larger one.

$$65 - 40 = 25$$

You are traveling about 25 miles per hour *below* the speed limit.

◀ *If you were in a car traveling at a speed of 47 mph, how would your speed compare to this speed limit sign?*

The term horsepower dates back to a time when the power for most forms of transportation was provided by horses.

Horsepower

Another term often applied to cars is horsepower. Horsepower is a unit of measure that was invented by an engineer named James Watt. More specifically, it is a unit for measuring work.

A car, for instance, is designed to move, but in order to move, it has to carry its own weight. The heavier a car is, the more work the engine has to do. Horsepower measures the amount of power a car can produce against its own load. So-called "high performance" cars have a lot of horsepower in relation to their weight. This means that they can speed up more quickly than a car with low horsepower.

TRAINS

At one time, trains were the most popular form of long-distance travel in America.

Trains are not as popular as they once were, but they are still a useful alternative to driving. The fact is, a journey by train can often take less time than the same journey by car. This is because a train can reach a greater **average** speed than a car.

This photo of a steam locomotive dates from the 1920s, just around the time when cars were becoming popular.

An average is a number that represents a group of numbers. If you are told that a car is traveling at an average speed of 45 mph, that doesn't mean that the car is always traveling at 45 mph. Sometimes it might be traveling faster than 45 mph, sometimes slower. Rather, the idea of average speed is that at any given time the speed of the car is *about* 45 mph.

A train can often reach a greater average speed than that of a car, partially because there are no obstacles in the way. Remember, there are a lot of cars in the world. Sometimes they get in each others' way, and the result is a traffic jam.

If this train maintains an average speed of 80 mph, how long will it take to make a trip of 3,750 miles?

Let's do some math to compare train travel and car travel. Imagine a journey between two cities—Los Angeles, California, and Chicago, Illinois. The **approximate** distance between these two cities is 2,000 miles.

First, let's focus on completing this journey by car. About how long would it take you to travel from Los Angeles to Chicago if you went by car and your average speed was around 65 mph?

You can find out by dividing the number of miles (2,000) by the average speed (65 mph):

$$2000 \div 65 = 30.77$$

So, it would take about 30.77 hours to make that trip by car.

Now let's imagine doing that trip on a train with an average speed of 80 mph. How long would the trip from Los Angeles to Chicago take?

$$2000 \div 80 = 25$$

It would take about 25 hours to make that same journey by train. How many hours fewer is the train journey than the trip by car? You can find out by subtracting the smaller number from the larger number:

$$31 - 25 = 6$$

The same journey by train would take about six hours less.

Along with the time factor, there are many reasons why some people prefer trains to driving. First of all, trains create less pollution than cars and are therefore better for the environment. Trains also require less responsibility. For instance, you can take a nap on a train ride, which is something you absolutely *cannot* do when you're driving. Likewise, in a car you would have to stop to get something to eat, while many trains have a café car.

In terms of speed, though, both trains and cars are left in the dust by *planes.*

Buses

They might not be as convenient as owning a car, and they aren't as much fun as trains or planes, but buses are a convenient way to transport large amounts of people over short distances.

You are probably already familiar with buses. Maybe you even take one to get to and from school. Unless you live in a big city, though, you might not know that buses are also a common form of **metropolitan** transportation.

Unfortunately, buses are subject to the same traffic jams as cars are. They are also expensive to operate because they require a lot of fuel. Typically, a car can outrun a bus, since a bus has to carry a much greater weight than a car going at a **comparable** speed. And because a city bus is a public service, the bus will stop every few blocks to pick up and discharge passengers.

A photo of Grand Central Station, New York City. When taking a form of transportation like a train or a plane, you should always arrive a little early to make sure you don't miss your ride.

PLANES

Planes are the most popular mode of passenger travel available today. This is largely due to the incredible speed at which travel is possible in a plane. Compared to the time it takes to get somewhere in a train or a car, plane travel takes place in the blink of an eye.

Jet planes are the most efficient, and popular, form of transportation today.

To demonstrate, let's plan another imaginary trip. This time, the journey will take you from Los Angeles, California, on the West Coast of the United States, to New York City, New York, on the East Coast of the United States. The distance between these two cities is roughly 3,000 miles.

First of all, let's calculate how long it would take to make that trip in a car traveling at an average speed of 65 mph:

$$3000 \div 65 = 46.15$$

So, a journey from Los Angeles to New York City by automobile would take about 46 hours.

You may have heard the phrase "the shortest distance between two points is a straight line." This is an important point, because in terms of a train trip, it isn't possible to go from Los Angeles to New York City in a straight line. Currently, the only way to make this trip would be to travel from Los Angeles to Chicago, and then from Chicago to New York City. For the purposes of this demonstration, though, let's pretend that you could travel directly from Los Angeles to New York City in a train going at an average speed of 80 mph. How long would it take to make that journey?

$$3000 \div 80 = 37.5$$

The journey from Los Angeles to New York City by train would take about 37 to 38 hours, which is a slight improvement over the 46-hour trip via car.

Now let's consider a plane. For the purposes of this example, imagine that the plane is a Boeing 747 aircraft. A Boeing 747 is capable of an average speed of about *560 mph*. How long would it take to fly from Los Angeles to New York City at that speed?

$$3{,}000 \div 560 = 5.35$$

So, to travel from Los Angeles to New York City in a plane only takes about five hours!

Now let's compare all three of our results:

CAR = 46.15 hours

TRAIN = 37.5 hours

PLANE = 5.35 hours

Using these numbers, how much faster is the journey from Los Angeles to New York City by plane compared to a car? To find out, just subtract the smaller number from the larger number:

$$46.15 - 5.35 = 40.8$$

The trip from Los Angeles to New York City in a plane takes about 41 hours *less* than the same trip in a car!

And what about the train versus the plane? What kind of an improvement is that?

$$37.5 - 5.35 = 32.15$$

The trip from Los Angeles to New York City in a plane takes about 32 hours *less* than the same trip on a train!

Now you understand why plane travel is so popular!

Planes have no need for roads and can simply fly over bodies of water.

Plane travel has other advantages as well. One thing that cars, trains, and even a person on foot can't deal with very well is water. Did you know that water covers about 70% of the earth's surface? When you think about that, the difficulties that water presents for travel become obvious. You can't just drive a car or a train through water. And unless you are superhuman, you can't really swim across an entire ocean either.

For planes, though, water is no problem. They just fly over it. Planes have made fast international travel—travel from one continent to another—possible.

24
23
22
21
20
19
18
17
16
15

For a long time, the most popular method of international travel was by boat. Boats are still used today, particularly for shipping purposes. However, they aren't used very much for passenger travel anymore. Again, this is because planes are simply quicker than boats, mainly because boats experience so much **resistance** from the water. A journey from America to Europe takes days on a boat. A plane can travel that same distance in a matter of hours.

Although planes are very fast, there is still room for improvement. That quest for a faster trip is exactly what led to the development of **supersonic** planes. Supersonic means traveling faster than the speed of sound.

!

Propellers

The planes you are used to seeing today are mostly jet aircraft. Before jets, though, planes had propellers.

If your family owns a boat you already know a little about propellers. A propeller is a device that looks like the blade of a fan. As you may have already guessed from the name, a propeller is a machine that propels, or pushes, a craft through a substance like water or air.

Propeller aircraft were slowly replaced because, compared to jet engines, propellers are fairly slow. You can still see propeller aircraft for yourself though, by visiting a museum of transportation or watching old movies. There are still some small propeller planes in use today. And helicopters use propellers, even though their propellers are located on the top and in the back instead of out front!

Boats were once an extremely popular form of passenger travel. Today, however, they are mainly used for shipping goods.

SOUND AND LIGHT

That's right. Sound *travels*.

It might seem hard to believe, but sound is just waves of air. Unlike, say, water, you can't see air—but it *is* there, and it moves at an incredible rate of speed.

How fast is sound? Sound travels at 1,100 feet per second.

You cannot see sound waves, but they behave in much the same way as the water waves pictured here. ▶

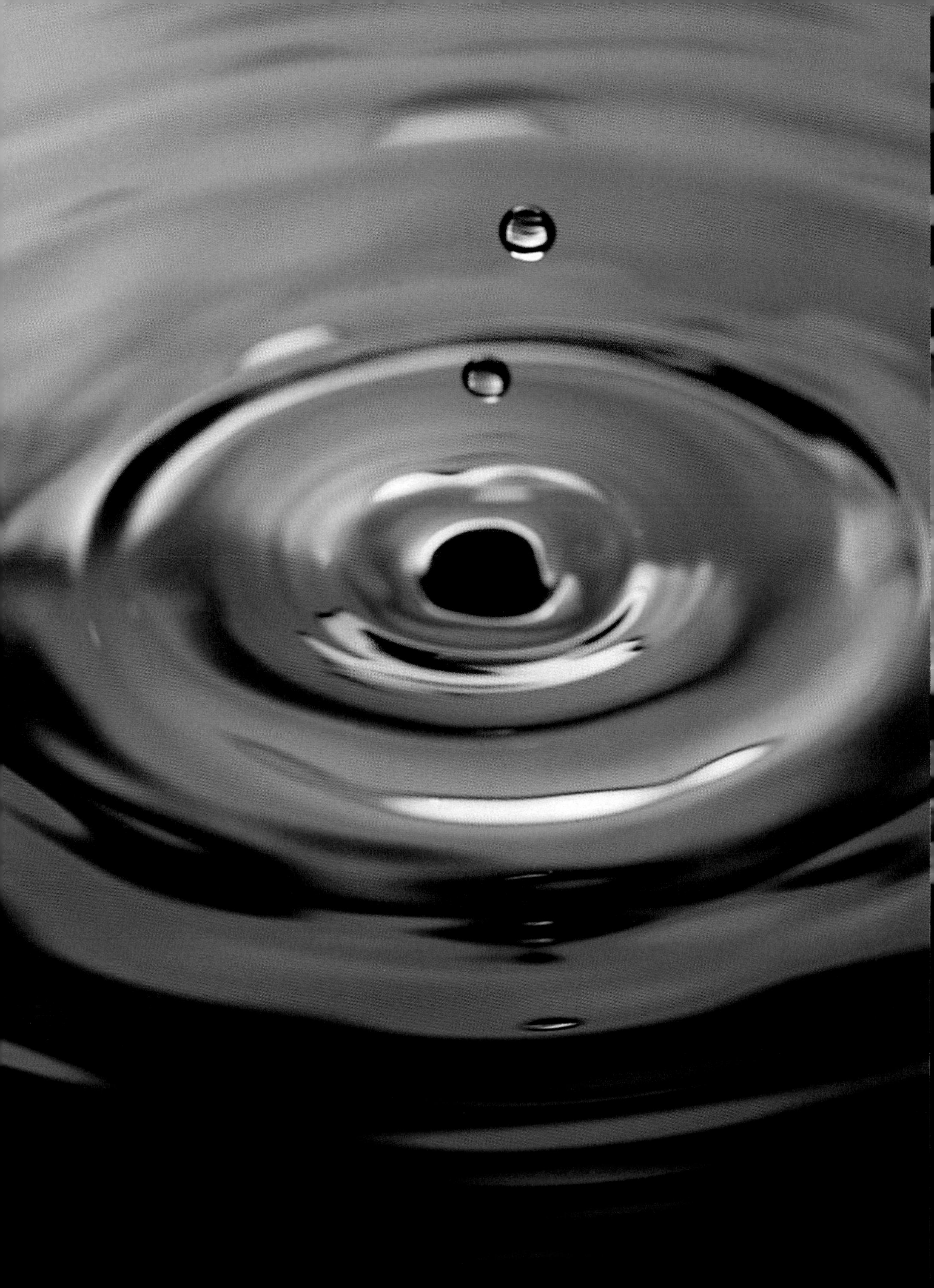

Imagine that you and a friend are standing in a large, open field. You are exactly one mile apart. If you were to make a loud noise, like the beep of a horn, how long would it take for that sound to reach your friend?

To find out, you need to divide the distance between you and your friend (one mile / 5,280 feet) by the speed of sound (1,100 feet per second):

$$5280 \div 1100 = 4.8$$

So it would take about five seconds for your friend to hear the beep of the horn.

Even the speed of sound though, seems slow compared to the speed of light. Light travels at an incredible 186,000 miles per second!

It takes about eight minutes for sunlight to reach the earth. If it was 4:30 p.m. when this photo was taken, at what time did the sunlight pictured here begin its journey?

Such a rate of speed might seem impossible. But if you think about it, it happens every day. For instance, the rays of light created by the sun have to travel to earth.

How long does it take for the light created by the sun to reach the earth?

You can find out, but get ready, because you're going to be dealing with some very big numbers here.

The distance from the sun to the earth is about 93 million miles. Or:

93,000,000 miles

Meanwhile, light travels at 186,000 miles per second. In order to find out how long it takes sunlight to reach the earth, you have to divide the distance from the sun to the earth (93,000,000 miles) by the speed of light:

$$93{,}000{,}000 \div 186{,}000 = 500 \text{ seconds}$$

To convert that number into minutes, divide 500 seconds by the number of seconds in one minute (60):

$$500 \div 60 = 8.3$$

Therefore, it takes a little more than eight minutes for a ray of sunlight to travel across space to the earth!

Sonic Boom

When a supersonic aircraft reaches top speed, it produces a sonic boom, a kind of noise produced by the waves of air the aircraft creates.

You already know that sound waves travel in much the same way that water waves do. Have you ever thrown a pebble into a pond? Then you have seen that waves travel in circles. They start from the center of the disturbance and then spread out.

But what happens if waves are created by a craft that is moving faster than the waves themselves? In that case, the craft—a speedboat, for instance—creates what is called a wake, or a big, single wave formed by a number of smaller waves. And, since the craft is traveling faster than the waves, the wake actually appears a few seconds after the craft has passed. That is exactly what a sonic boom is. It is the wake created by the airwaves disturbed by a supersonic jet.

SPACE PLANES

What kinds of travel will people be able to experience in the future? How much more efficient will those forms of travel be than what we have now? And how can travel speeds possibly improve?

Remember that you learned about two different forms of resistance, including the resistance created by water, which boats have to cope with, and air resistance, which planes have to deal with. Take away both types of resistance, though, and the potential for faster speeds is incredible.

The reason why the surface of the earth appears to glow is because of our planet's atmosphere. The atmosphere is what causes wind resistance for planes. By leaving the earth's atmosphere, space planes will be able to travel at incredible speeds. ▶

That is the concept behind the "space planes," which are considered to be the next big development in travel and transportation. Space planes will actually leave the earth's atmosphere in order to travel great distances without air resistance. It is estimated that space planes will be capable of travel speeds up to 15 times the speed of sound. How fast is that?

You can find out by multiplying the speed of sound (1,100 feet per second) by 15:

$$1,100 \times 15 = 16,500$$

So space planes could potentially travel at speeds up to 16,500 feet per second! Can you find out how many miles per second that is?

$$16,500 \div 5,280 = 3.125$$

About three miles a second!

But what does that mean in practical terms? How long would it take a space plane, for instance, to travel the journey from New York City to Great Britain?

To find out, you need to divide the number of miles between New York City and Great Britain (3,500) by the number of miles a space plane can cover in one second (3.125):

$$3{,}500 \div 3.125 = 1{,}120$$

So a space plane could travel from New York City to Great Britain in about 1,120 seconds. How many minutes is that?

To find out, divide the number of seconds (1,120) by the number of seconds in one minute (60):

$$1{,}120 \div 60 = 18$$

Eighteen minutes! Pretty amazing, isn't it?

Space planes won't be that efficient, though. They'll need extra time to take off and leave the atmosphere. Likewise, re-entering the atmosphere will require extra time. Still, even with those factors considered, you're still looking at a journey of about one hour!

CONCLUSION

Have you ever heard the expression, “time is money?” Do you know what it means?

It is a phrase that describes the importance of time in relation to work. The amount of money a person can make is determined by, among other things, how quickly they can do their work.

The point is, we live in a fast culture, and it is only getting faster. That is why the quest for ever-faster modes of transportation will continue.

Time is money!

If space planes do become the dominant form of transportation, the only other possible improvement would be some method of **instantaneous** travel. One possibility would be the kind of travel you see in science fiction films, where people are "teleported" from one location to another by use of lasers that deconstruct and reassemble their bodies. Such a mode of transportation would bring people very close to traveling at the speed of light.

But everyone knows that people can't travel at the speed of light. That's impossible!

True. But people once said that about flying…

You'll just have to wait and see!

THE METRIC SYSTEM

We actually have two systems of weights and measure in the United States. Quarts, pints, gallons, ounces, and pounds are all units of the U.S. Customary System, also known as the English System.

The other system of measurement, and the only one sanctioned by the United States Government, is the metric system, which is also known as the International System of Units. French scientists developed the metric system in the 1790s. The basic unit of measurement in the metric system is the meter, which is about one ten-millionth the distance from the North Pole to the equator.

A metal bar used to represent the length of the standard meter was even created. This bar was replaced in the 1980s, though, when scientists changed the standard of measurement for the meter to a portion of the distance traveled by light in a vacuum.

Space planes and teleports won't be a reality for several years. Until then, what's your favorite form of travel?

Most of the world uses the metric system. In terms of travel, this usually means that distances are measured not in miles, but in kilometers. One mile is equal to 1.621 kilometers.

The calculations for metric measurement are a simple matter of multiplication. For instance, if a distance is 20 miles, how many kilometers is it?

$$1.621 \times 20 = 32.42$$

20 miles is equal to about 32.42 kilometers!

If a car is traveling at 50 mph, how fast is it going in kilometers per hour (kph)?

$$50 \times 1.621 = 81.05$$

The car is traveling a little over 81 kph!

GLOSSARY

approximate – not exact, an estimate

average – a number used to represent a group of numbers

comparable – similar

dashboard – a panel located beneath a car's windshield on the inside; includes controls and instruments

efficient – something that operates without a great deal of waste, expense, or need for effort

escalators – mechanical stairways

exercise – physical activity done on a regular basis to keep the body conditioned

highway – a large public road, often with several lanes; used to connect towns and cities

instantaneous – instantly, without interruption

metropolitan – a city area

multiples – the result of multiplying a single number by a series of other numbers

multiplication – a method for adding large groups of numbers

notches – marks or symbols used to represent something like a word or letter

recreation – activity for fun

residential – an area where people live

resistance – a force that slows down or prevents motion

speed – distance traveled in a specific amount of time

speed limit – the highest speed at which a car is allowed to travel in a particular area

speedometer – an instrument that indicates the speed at which a car is traveling

stride length – the distance a person covers in a single step

supersonic – faster than the speed of sound (1,110 feet per second)

transportation – a method of traveling, or getting from one place to another

travel – to go from one place to another

Further Reading

Axelrod, Amy. *Pigs on the Move: Fun With Math and Travel.* Simon & Schuster, 1999.

Braybrooks, Anne. *Math Mania: Travel Games To Go.* Grosset & Dunlap, 1998.

Zeman, Anne and Kate Kelly. *Everything You Need To Know About Math Homework*. Scholastic, 1994.

Websites to Visit

http://abcnews.go.com/sections/tech/Geek/geek001123.html
ABC News – How a Car's Speedometer Works

http://auto.howstuffworks.com/horsepower.htm
How Stuff Works – Horsepower

www.amtrak.com
Amtrak

http://auto.howstuffworks.com/space-plane.htm
How Stuff Works – How Space Planes Will Work

INDEX

About The Author

Kieran Walsh has written a variety of children's nonfiction books, primarily on historical and social studies topics, including the recent Rourke series *Holiday Celebrations* and *Countries In the News*. He divides his time between upstate New York and New York City.